# CONVERSATIONS
## *with a*
## *Moonflower*

# CHRIS HALL

BONNEVILLE BOOKS
SPRINGVILLE, UTAH

What others are saying about
*Conversations with a Moonflower*

"*Conversations with a Moonflower* speaks to your soul and touches your heart. Tender and insightful, this book is filled with life lessons and wisdom that allow the reader to look inside and recognize the power and potential we all have inside of us. Beautifully written, this is one book that readers will connect with and treasure, a book that will be read over and over. New author Chris Hall provides a fresh voice and message that will leave you feeling uplifted."

—Michele Ashman Bell, Author of
*An Unexpected Love* and *A Modest Proposal*

"A wise, warm, and wonderful book—a gentle reminder that in a high-tech, hurry-up world, there is value in pausing to enjoy the presence of loved ones and the simple beauties of life. This book is a gift, with an important and needed message. Give it to every busy person you know!"

—Carrie Maxwell Wrigley, LCSW

# To Duane

"I DO LOVE NOTHING IN THE WORLD SO WELL AS YOU."

—WILLIAM SHAKESPEARE AND ME

ISBN 13: 978-1-59955-795-3

Published by Bonneville Books, an imprint of Cedar Fort, Inc.
2373 W. 700 S., Springville, UT 84663
Distributed by Cedar Fort, Inc., www.cedarfort.com

LIBRARY OF CONGRESS CATALOGING-IN-PUBLICATION DATA

Hall, Chris, 1949 November 9- , author.
  Conversations with a moonflower / Chris Hall.
      p. cm.
  Summary: An Amish woman gives her deceased neighbor's family a moonflower,
  which changes their lives for the better.
  ISBN 978-1-59955-795-3
  1. Moonflower--Fiction. 2. Amish--Fiction. I. Title.
  PS3608.A54683C66 2011
  813'.6--dc22
                        2010053210

Front cover photograph courtesy of Cliff Hutson
Back cover moonflower photograph courtesy of Shauna Hall Farnsworth
Illustrations by Megan Whittier and Danie Romrell
Cover and page design by Megan Whittier
Cover design © 2011 by Lyle Mortimer
Edited by Heather Holm

Printed in the United States of America

10  9  8  7  6  5  4  3  2  1

Printed on acid-free paper

# ACKNOWLEDGMENTS

I have come to better understand the meaning of "generosity of heart" while writing this book, since I have been the recipient of the extraordinary skill, kindness, interest, and assistance from several valued friends.

I'm not sure this book would have been published without the assistance of LaRene Gaunt, an exceptional editor and author, who generously shared her editing skills and was a major source of encouragement and support. The words "thank you" are woefully inadequate; nevertheless, thank you my dear friend.

Special thanks also to another gifted writer and

friend, Michele Ashman Bell, who has been so kind and supportive as she walked me through the many steps of getting a book published and patiently answered my endless questions. I also express love and appreciation to my mother-in-law, Manell Hall, who was one of the first to edit the book. Your insights were invaluable.

I express my heartfelt appreciation to the wonderfully talented and creative staff at Cedar Fort Publishing, specifically to my editor Heather Holm, acquisitions editor Shersta Gatica, production manager Jennifer Fielding, and designer Megan Whittier. You have made this such a great experience for me.

And last, the best of all the game, thank you to my beloved husband and children for your continual love and encouragement. You are my greatest joys on earth.

# CONTENTS

# Contents

## PART I

# A New Gathering Place

# The Gathering

It was almost dark when our caravan approached the top of Seager Hill and we caught our first glimpse of the familiar small white structure partially hidden in the trees. We began the singsong chant we had sung a hundred times as children. "I see Grandma's schoolhouse! I see Grandma's schoolhouse!" Then we saw it—the one-room schoolhouse where our grandmother taught until she was seventy-four years old. As we passed the school, we knew we were almost to Grandma's.

When we cleared the last hill and saw our family farm before us, I was filled with the same joy and anticipation I had felt countless times as a child. We were at Grandma's—we were home.

The white clapboard farmhouse sat partway down the hill and was surrounded by the gently rolling hills of Cattaraugus County, New York. Located in the southwestern part of New York State, this was farm country. Beautiful farms, many of them belonging to the Amish, dotted the landscape in every direction. As we pulled into the driveway, a flood of emotion filled me, and I knew this trip would be unlike any I had experienced.

Filled with memories, mystery, and forbidden rooms, Grandma's farmhouse was always like a museum to us as children. The farm had been in our family since the 1840s. My grandmother was born there in 1888. She later married, and she and my grandfather raised their two children there. Grandpa died in 1947, and Grandma lived the rest of her life in the home where she was born. She passed away in her own bed in May 1993 at the age of 105. The home passed to our father, and with his death in 2001, we knew the time had come to sell this beloved home and land that had been our family's gathering place all our lives.

And so my two sisters, my brother, and I gathered there one last time. We traveled across the country, bringing our spouses and some of our children to help us clean, sort, and eliminate the belongings of more than a century of living.

My husband and I and two of our children drove from Utah, towing a small trailer so we could take home my grandmother's cherished china cabinet. I knew that my sisters and brother and I would divide other treasures among us, but I never imagined that the most priceless treasure I would take home from that trip was something that didn't belong to my grandmother. It would, however, travel back across the country with me in her old, blue enamel dishpan. And it would change my life.

# The Amish

*I*awoke early the next morning to the familiar sound of horse hooves clip-clopping down the road. Grandma's property was surrounded by Amish farms, and the Amish would pass by in their buggies and wagons throughout the day. Even though it was not yet 6:30 in the morning, I had already heard several buggies go past the house.

No one else was awake, so I allowed myself a few more minutes to rest before beginning a hard day of cleaning. I always loved waking up at Grandma's, particularly in the summer months when the windows were open and you could breathe in that indescribable smell of country air. The only thing missing that morning was waking to the smell of bacon and eggs cooking on Grandma's wood-burning stove. Another horse-drawn wagon passed the house, and I wondered who it was and where they were going so early in the morning.

The Amish were dear to our hearts. They had extended their friendship and many kindnesses to our family over the years, especially to my grandmother, who continued to live in her home for more than forty-five years following the death of my grandfather.

The Amish believe in remaining separate from the world, physically and socially. They do not have electricity or telephones in their homes, but they are allowed to use phones, so on many occasions they would come to my grandmother's home to use hers, often staying awhile to visit.

Grandma started teaching school when she was fourteen years old and taught well past the age that most teachers retire. In her later years, she taught the Amish children in their one-room schoolhouse, located a half mile up the road from the farm. Some of the farmers who stopped by to visit with her were former students now raising families of their own.

The simplicity with which the Amish lived always fascinated me. Their homes were plain and unadorned and often remained unpainted, but inside they were immaculate. The wood floors throughout the homes were spotless, and the furnishings, though simple, were certainly adequate. All of the children I met or observed seemed well mannered and polite. As we drove by their farms, we would often see the older children out working in the fields with their father, and the younger ones stayed close by their mother, who was hanging clothes out to dry or working in the vegetable garden. I have no memory of ever seeing them hurry. They always seemed to have time to stop and visit for a few minutes, and there was a peaceful calm and serenity about them that I had longed for most of my adult life.

They spoke quietly to us and to one another. Occasionally I heard an Amish man raise his voice, but usually at a team of horses not following his lead. I recall numerous times when we were visiting Grandma that I listened in on a conversation between my dad and an Amish neighbor.

I loved hearing them speak with their strong German accents and hearing them say, "Ayah" when they agreed with you. It wasn't until I was much older that I noticed something else about the way they communicated. They seemed to really listen to what you were saying. When you finished speaking, they often paused a moment before answering, as if reflecting on what you had said.

So many things about the Amish were the opposite of my life. Little about me was relaxed or unhurried. I struggled from my earliest childhood with Attention Deficit Disorder, and I always seemed to be moving. More often than not, I had a multitude of disconnected thoughts racing through my mind all at the same time, and I often answered my children before they finished their question. Being at Grandma's farm always had a calming effect on me, and one of the best parts of a trip was when a horse and buggy pulled into the yard.

The Amish family we knew best was the Yoder

family who lived about a quarter of a mile down the hill from Grandma's. Jacob Yoder and his family moved to Conewango in 1951 and purchased the farm that had once belonged to my great-aunt Rhelda. They soon befriended my widowed grandmother and often stopped to check on her, especially in bad weather.

Even though the Yoders were Grandma's closest neighbor, she had no way to contact them if she needed help. They eventually set up a system for her to get their attention. Grandma put a red light bulb in a small lamp that resembled an old-fashioned candlestick and placed the lamp on the table in front of the parlor window facing the Yoder's. If she turned on the light, regardless of the weather, Jacob or one of his sons would soon appear at her door. That small lamp became one of my most treasured possessions, a frequent reminder of our dear Amish friends.

Following Grandma's death, my father arranged with the funeral home to have a viewing for Grandma in her own parlor the day before the public viewing. He knew the Amish would want to pay their respects in private. Our family was deeply touched when the schoolteacher, who now taught in Grandma's one-room schoolhouse, led the procession of Amish children down the road to Grandma's home to pay their respects to a former teacher they had never met but who had taught some of their parents.

Throughout that day the families came, tying their buggies to the huge maple trees that lined the driveway. At one point my sister touched my arm and nodded toward the dining room. Our grandmother's lovely dining room table was covered with men's straw hats. It would have made a stunning black-and-white photo, and we all wanted to reach for our cameras but knew better. We were taught from our earliest childhood that the Amish do not want their picture taken. It is part of their beliefs, and to do so would be disrespectful to them and a great disappointment to my grandmother. So I took a snapshot in my mind, and to this day, it is one of my favorites in a private collection that I keep in my heart.

Another wagon passed the house and quickly brought me out of my reverie. I could have lain there another hour remembering the fun and adventures we had as children when we were at Grandma's farm. But it was time to get up and get the day started since we had only four days to accomplish two weeks' worth of work. This would be our greatest and last adventure at the farm, and I didn't want to waste one minute of it.

# We Begin

I sat up and looked around the room and laughed out loud. We were all in sleeping bags that completely covered the floor of Grandma's front room and parlor. Suitcases, duffle bags, adults, and children were wall-to-wall, and it was almost impossible to get out of the room without stepping on someone. My sister Joan heard me stirring and opened her eyes. She looked around the room and then back at me, and we both burst out laughing.

"Okay," she said as she got up, "we can do this," and we began the process of getting everyone up and organizing the day ahead.

Our first need was water. Our Amish friend, Jacob,

had checked the pump on the well a month earlier and wrote to my brother Bill that he didn't think it was working. Bill and my husband looked at it as soon as we arrived. Our fears were confirmed—the pump wasn't working, and it would take days to get the necessary parts to fix it. Since fourteen of us were at the farm with no running water, the men drove down the hill to Jacob's farm. They returned with four large stainless steel milk cans filled with water from Jacob's well that were refilled countless times over the next four days.

My sister Nancy took over the job of feeding us for the week. A wonderful cook, she had inherited our grandmother's ability to make an incredible meal out of very little. She came prepared with the staples necessary to prepare meals for the next four days and made us feel like Grandma was still there.

Before long the familiar smell of bacon, eggs, and biscuits filled the house, and we came up with a plan of action while we sat around the dining room table eating. We decided we would all work on the large areas together, and as teams in the smaller rooms. If we found anything we deemed noteworthy, or if we had questions as to something's value, we would share it with the group. Otherwise, it was up to each of us to use our best judgment in deciding what to keep and what to discard.

My brother had ordered a sixteen-foot dumpster, which was delivered that morning. Jacob came around noon with one of his large wagons and pulled it up to the back porch. He said that if we found things we didn't want but didn't want to throw away, we could put them on his wagon and he would take care of them. His criterion was simple: "If you don't want something but think it's worth a nickel, put it on the wagon." We filled the wagon three times in the days ahead and often wondered what he did with all of it.

We started in Grandma's infamous "back room" and the attic room above it. The back room, located behind the kitchen, had at one time been our grandfather's workroom, and the walls were lined with workbenches and old woodworking tools. As the years went by, Grandpa's workroom became a storage room, packed with boxes stacked six feet high and filled with broken objects that Grandma must have hoped would be repaired someday.

In the far corner of the back room was a set of rickety stairs that led to the attic. When we were children, Grandma forbade us to go up in the attic (although we did sneak up there a few times). As we climbed the stairs that morning, I couldn't get over the feeling that I was a kid again, getting away with something.

The attic was filled with broken furniture, old pieces of farm equipment, trunks, and dozens of boxes of books, papers, and keepsakes. We found trunks filled with old clothes and unfinished dresses and shirts and wondered for whom they were intended.

As we opened box after box of old documents, letters, and newspaper clippings, we had a tendency to want to sit and read through every paper. Eventually we decided to keep the boxes of papers we wanted to carefully go through, take them back to my sister's home in upstate New York, and store them in *her* attic. Knowing the papers wouldn't be thrown away was all it took to get me back to work. Box by box, we slowly emptied the attic.

We found dozens of old maple syrup pails hanging from the rafters throughout the attic. Cattaraugus County was at one time maple syrup country, and Grandpa tapped the maple trees on his property every year in early spring. We decided that each of us would take a pail home for each one of our children.

We discovered old steel milking pails and pieces of farm equipment that had been stored in the attic since before we were born, and it was fun to imagine what life was like when our father was a boy.

On the second day, we cleaned out Grandma's kitchen cupboards, her two china cabinets, and the buffet. We piled dishes, pots and pans, china, and glassware all over the dining room on her large table, desks, and side tables. We then began the process of deciding what was worth keeping and who would take what treasures home.

We agreed we would take turns choosing what we wanted, one item each turn, starting with the oldest. Even though we all had other family members there, we decided that only the four of us could actually choose an item. My brother Bill often had us in stitches when someone chose an item that he wanted. He would say, "But Dad told me I could have that." Over and over again it became our comic relief when Bill would tell us that Dad had given him just about everything, including, at times, things that were our own possessions.

It was hot, dirty, exhausting work. We relished the moments when someone found a treasure and we could sit down for a few minutes and reminisce.

On the third day we moved upstairs into the bedrooms. Of special interest to me was the back bedroom, piled high with trunks, old clothes, and keepsakes of my grandmother and great-grandmother.

In one dresser drawer I found two left-hand leather gloves that had belonged to my Grandfather. They were a stirring reminder of the determination and capability of the human spirit. My grandpa, while still in his twenties, lost his right forearm in a piece of farm equipment. I remember asking my father once if Grandpa had been left- or right-handed. He laughed softly and then said matter-of-factly, "Well, he was right-handed. But after he lost his right arm, he was left-handed." For the rest of his life, Grandpa ran a dairy farm using his left hand and a hook.

In the late afternoon, a horse-drawn buggy came into the yard. Nancy and I were in the dining room bagging clothes when we heard a knock on the front door. We looked up, and through the screen door we saw Jacob's son Samuel and his wife, Marissa. We welcomed them and were delighted when they presented us with a large tray of warm, homemade, glazed doughnuts.

As we visited with our Amish friends, Marissa said, "If you girls are done with your work by about 8:45 tonight, you could come down to the house and watch our moonflower bloom."

"What is a moonflower?" several of us asked in unison.

"Oh," she replied. "You must come and see. You've never seen anything like it. They are plants with flowers that only open at dusk—and when they do, they open right before your eyes in just a few seconds." Then, almost as an afterthought, she added quietly, "It will amaze you."

Joan and I thanked her and said we would try to come. After we closed the front door, we looked at each other and sighed. What had we gotten ourselves into? We were so dirty from the cleaning and were utterly exhausted. We would have to clean up before we went to visit. We decided to see how much energy we had after dinner.

As I continued working, the thought of going to Marissa's to see her plant bloom wouldn't leave me alone. The Amish rarely invited us to their homes, and I felt like my grandmother would want us to go. And so, a little after 8:00 p.m., Joan and I got cleaned up. At the last minute our teenagers decided they wanted to go and jumped into the van just before we left. When we drove out of Grandma's driveway that warm July evening, I could not have imagined that what I was about to see would bring my family joy, delight, and a gathering place at my own home for many years to come.

# The Moonflower

As we pulled into the yard, Marissa came out of the house to greet us. "I'm glad you could come," she said softly. "You're just in time."

We followed her around the corner of the house and saw several of her children standing near the edge of her flower garden, intently watching a large plant that spanned a distance of more than six feet. "It's starting!" one of them said. When we got closer we realized that it wasn't one plant, but probably fifteen or twenty separate plants, each about eighteen inches across and eighteen inches tall.

I was taken aback by the appearance of the plant.

From Marissa's description I had expected something beautiful, with large silky leaves, but this looked more like a massive weed. The leaves actually reminded me of dandelion leaves, only much longer. Some of the leaves were eighteen inches long, and at the most, about one-half inch wide. Each plant had many leaves, all growing upward, and throughout the plant I noticed slender stalks protruding from the base. The stalks were at different stages of development. Many were barely peeking through the leaves while others were six, twelve, or eighteen inches tall. Each stalk had a pod on the end. The pods on the tallest stalks were well defined and much fuller than the shorter ones.

Marissa pointed to the tallest and fullest pods. "Keep your eye on these," she said. "They are the ones that will bloom tonight. When they get ready to open, you will notice that they begin to shake a little, almost like they are pulling energy up from their roots to gather enough strength to open. You can spot the ones that are going to open next because the pod will split somewhere near the top, and you will see the yellow flower underneath peeking through."

One of her children called our attention to a pod that had split. We all moved over to it, and her children stepped back so we could see. Just as Marissa had said, the pod, which was about two-and-a-half inches long, had split from top to bottom. Then, as we watched, it split again on the other side. The yellow beneath it was bulging, and in an instant the entire green wrapping of the pod broke loose. All that remained was the yellow bud, which was still tightly wrapped. One of Marissa's youngest children, a little girl about three or four years old, jumped up and down and clapped her hands as the yellow flower opened. It was like watching time-lapse photography, for in no more than ten seconds the flower went from being tightly wrapped to being completely open. I couldn't believe what I saw. It was beautiful! The bright yellow flower, which measured about three inches across, had four petals that opened until they were almost flat.

I wanted to see one open again, and I only had to wait a few seconds before another child called out, "This one!" We moved up and down the length of the plant, watching as one pod after another opened.

Our teenagers thought it was "so cool." The Amish children were grinning as our teenagers became totally absorbed in watching the blossoms open. They exclaimed, "Check this out!", "Awesome!", and "No way!"

I was completely fascinated by this plant's unusual appearance and great beauty. Since the moonflower only bloomed at dusk, I wondered how many people would pass by it during the day, never knowing what they were missing. If I had seen one of them growing in my garden, I would have pulled it out immediately, thinking it a giant weed. But this was no weed—it was magnificent!

I was captivated by Marissa's children and their joy as each pod bloomed. Sometimes so many pods were opening at once that our eyes darted from one plant to the next. The whole show lasted about fifteen minutes, and our delight in this wonderful discovery was obvious.

Marissa told us that the flowers stay open all through

the night, but they begin to wilt when the sun's full morning rays touch them. She said that by afternoon the blooms will have completely wilted and the stems will fall over. "But," she promised, "There will be new ones that night to take their place."

It was now completely dark. We knew we should go so that Marissa could get her children into bed, but I didn't want to leave. I wanted to sit down quietly for a few minutes by her moonflowers and process the myriad thoughts that were spinning through my head.

While my sister and Marissa were talking, I slowly walked to the end of the garden. I leaned over a plant and whispered, "You are amazing."

For a brief moment I thought I heard a voice whisper, "As are you," but no one was there.

I looked up and noticed that Joan and Marissa were walking slowly toward the van. I caught up with them as Marissa said, "When are you girls leaving for home?"

"Tomorrow," Joan replied. "We're hoping to be on our way by noon."

"Well, if you would like to stop by in the morning

before you leave, I can have a moonflower plant ready for you so you can each take one home."

We were touched by her thoughtful gesture and said we would most certainly stop by before we left. I had wanted to ask her earlier if she could part with one but thought it might not be appropriate to ask. I could not have been more pleased with her offer.

We climbed in the van, and as our headlights came on, I noticed several of her children shyly peeking at us from around the corner of the house. We waved out the windows to them, and they waved back.

My heart was filled with emotion as we drove up the road, and I was having a hard time processing my thoughts and feelings. What on earth had just happened to me? It was a plant, for heaven's sake! With the exception of the bright yellow blooms, it looked more like a weed than anything you would purposely put in a garden. But this mysterious plant had captivated me, and I couldn't wait to tell the others what we had seen.

When we arrived, everyone was in the front room watching TV. "So how was the plant?" someone asked.

We tried to explain how thrilling it was and to describe our amazement when the pods split and the blossoms unfolded before our eyes, but they hadn't seen or felt what we had, and they didn't understand. They said all the right things to show their enthusiasm, but their eyes kept glancing from the TV to us and back to the screen again.

We sat down for a few minutes and joined them, but I wasn't paying attention to the show. I couldn't get over the delight I felt as I watched the plant bloom in the twilight.

Even though there were things about the Amish's serene and uncluttered lifestyle that I had always longed for, I sometimes felt sad for them. Without electricity and cars and modern conveniences, it seemed they were missing out on so many experiences that make life rich and full. My sister and I joked as we were driving to Marissa's house that the reason they got so excited over a moonflower blooming is because they don't have television, but I don't recall ever seeing a TV show that produced such a profound and immediate effect on me.

As I got ready for bed that night, my mind wandered to my own home in Utah with its running hot and cold water, telephone, and electricity that provided my air conditioning, bright lights, and invaluable computer. Just before I drifted off to sleep, I thought again about Marissa and her home in Conewango Valley and wondered which of us really possessed the truest comforts of life.

# Time to Leave

Late the next morning, while the others finished packing, Joan and I drove back to Marissa's. She had gone out early that morning, dug up a plant for each of us, and placed them in small boxes, being sure to pack plenty of dirt around each one to sustain them for the long trip ahead. She reassured us that they wouldn't require much attention once we got them home, just water and occasional fertilizer. She said that by the next summer we would have big plants of our own.

We thanked her again for all their help that week, and especially for introducing us to her plant. I didn't know when I would be back to that area again, and I felt as I did the night before, wanting to stay with Marissa a while longer but knowing it was time to leave. She walked us to the car as we said good-bye, and we drove back to the farm.

My family and I had a long trip ahead of us for the next few days, and we felt an urgency to get on the road as soon as possible. I looked around for a stronger container to take my moonflower home in, found Grandma's old blue enamel dishpan in the back room, and placed the plant in it. I went outside and got more dirt from the edge of grandma's old vegetable garden and packed it around the plant along with the dirt from Marissa's garden.

The trailer was packed and the back of our SUV was full, so I opened the back window and made a space for the dishpan, placing it near the window so the plant could get plenty of sunshine on the long trip home.

We all knew it was time to leave, but we were having trouble actually doing it. We kept going back into the house to see if there was anything else that we had left. We gathered on the front porch for a group picture in front of the home we had loved so much for so long. The bond between us had always been strong, but it had grown even stronger that week as we tenderly sorted through our family's past. Loving emotions filled the air as we said good-bye. Cousins tearfully embraced, my sisters and brother and I hugged again and again, and we finally got in our cars.

Like a caravan, one car after another, we pulled out of the driveway, drove up the road behind an Amish buggy, and headed back to our normal lives. It is said that you can't go back home again, but I'm not so sure about that anymore. For four hot, exhausting, wonderful days that July, we relived our past through grown-up eyes, and I regained a sense of childlike awe and wonder that I had not known in years.

# The Trip Home

For the next four days, we drove west, stopping occasionally at places of interest. One night, while we were driving, my daughter turned around in her seat to get something out of the back. "Mom!" she said incredulously, "Your moonflower bloomed!"

I couldn't believe it! A few minutes later we stopped for the night, and I couldn't wait to see it for myself. It had bloomed, in the car, in my grandmother's dishpan! I felt as if it were telling me that it was happy to be part of our family now as it traveled to its new home in the west.

When we finally arrived home, we decided to back the trailer into the garage for the night and unpack it the next morning. We unloaded our luggage from the car and I carried grandma's dishpan and my moonflower into the house. Too tired to plant it, I left it on the counter for the night.

I walked around my yard the next morning trying to decide where to put my moonflower. I decided the front corner of the house would be the perfect place, because it faced west and would get plenty of sun. I finally chose a spot in the flower bed, dug a hole, and added mulch to the soil before transplanting it. With great ceremony I placed it into the ground and lovingly covered the roots with rich, dark soil. "You'll be safe here," I whispered. "Dig your roots in deep."

I checked on it frequently over the next few weeks to be sure it was taking root. The leaves were green and looked healthy, but I knew it would be a shock to the plant to be transplanted in the heat of the summer. I was sure it would not bloom again that year. Fall came and the plant began to wither after the first frost. Then winter covered it with a foot of snow. When the spring thaw came, I was anxious to see how it weathered its first Utah winter. When the snow completely melted, I walked outside one afternoon to see how it looked.

I could see the brown, fibrous taproot protruding slightly above the ground, looking just as it had in November, but there were no visible signs of life, and I wondered if it had died. A few weeks later, to my great relief, I noticed a few tiny leaves growing out of the root. It was alive! As the days warmed, the plant began to grow, and within a month it was twelve inches across.

One night, at the end of May, my husband and I were out for the evening when one of my daughters called my cell phone. "Mom, I really think the moonflower is going to bloom tonight! One pod looks different! It's gotten really fat and it's a different color. Hurry home!"

We headed home and got there a few minutes before it bloomed. My husband had never seen one open before, and he was as captivated as we were by the experience. "Well isn't that something," he said quietly. "I've never seen anything like it."

It was days before another one bloomed, and then days again before the next. One night at dusk, a friend drove by our house and saw me and my daughter on our knees in front of the plant. She slowed down and called out the window, "What are you two doing—watching your flowers grow?"

We laughed and said, "Actually, we are! Come see!"

She parked and walked over and we told her about the moonflower. She sat down on the lawn and visited with us for a few minutes. Suddenly the stem started to shake.

"It's going to open!" my daughter shouted as once again a flower on our mysterious and wonderful plant opened before our eyes.

My friend leaned toward the plant, her eyes wide. She had a puzzled smile on her face. "Okay, seriously," she said, "that is the most amazing plant I have ever seen! Where did you get it?"

I told her the story and she seemed enchanted by it.

"Well," she said, "That's too far for me to go to get one. Can I come by your house from time to time and watch yours?"

I told her she was welcome to come and watch it anytime, whether we were home or not.

A few nights later I walked outside as the sun was setting to see if any blossoms would open that night. My friend and one of her teenage daughters were already on the lawn.

"I hope you don't mind that I brought my daughter," she said. "I've been telling the kids about it and she wanted to see it for herself."

"You are both always welcome," I assured her.

Within a few minutes one blossom opened. Her daughter was amazed. "Whoa!" she said, her eyes wide. "That is so cool." It didn't look like any more would open that night, but the teenage girl did not seem disappointed. She sat on the lawn and visited with her mom and me for about twenty minutes before they had to leave.

Several nights later my friend's daughter showed up with two of her friends, a full half hour before the plant usually bloomed, and rang our doorbell. "I came back to watch your moonflower," she said. "Is it okay that I brought my friends?"

"Anytime," I answered. "You are all always welcome." They sat down on the lawn, and I could hear them from my kitchen window, laughing and talking while waiting for the "show" to begin.

The next night I was out weeding the flower beds when a neighbor walked by. "Hey," she called to me, "what's this I hear about you having an Amish plant?"

I laughed. "It's our moonflower." I got up and walked her to the corner of the house and showed it to her.

"What time does it bloom?" she asked.

"Well, it doesn't bloom every night yet," I explained, "But it looks like it might tonight."

"What time?"

"If you're here a few minutes before nine you'll be in time," I replied.

When I went outside to check the plant a few hours later, she was already there with two of her children, along with another friend and her two girls. I smiled as I realized that my friends and I had spent more time visiting by my moonflower in the past week than we had in the last few months.

It was interesting to me that even after the plant opened at night, the teenagers seemed content to sit on the lawn and visit for a while with whoever was there. No one seemed to have a great need to get back to something. It was as if time slowed down and we had all been transported to another time and place.

Our moonflower conversations were leisurely. Many nights I would find myself, after a day of racing from one thing to the next, looking forward to sunset when my husband and I would go outside and do nothing but sit and visit with each other for the next thirty or forty minutes. Sometimes we were joined by friends while waiting for the plant to bloom.

One night, a friend and I sat talking long after the last pod opened. She was new to the moonflower and mentioned that many nights she had driven by and noticed seven or eight people gathered at the corner of our house, all looking intently at the ground. She wondered for weeks what was so interesting in my flower bed, but never stopped to ask. We talked about how many people had come to see it and how enjoyable it was in the cool of the summer evenings to sit and visit. I mentioned how several friends had commented that they thought they enjoyed the conversation almost as much as watching the moonflower open.

"It's a gathering place," my friend said at length. "You brought a gathering place home with you from the Amish."

# *If You Plant It, They Will Come*

S unday nights soon became the moonflower's big night. Our children and grandchildren often came for Sunday dinner, and no one ever wanted to leave before the plant bloomed. The grandchildren would sit on the lawn for half an hour or more, waiting for what they called "the moonflower show." They chased each other around the yard, did cartwheels and handstands, and often dragged all the lawn chairs around to the front yard so everyone could have a seat.

Friends driving by would see the crowd gathering and stop to see what was going on, often returning a few nights later with other friends. One Sunday night we had twenty-seven people all crowded together to watch our amazing plant.

My granddaughter suggested that we start baking cookies for the "moonflower party," and so one Sunday night after dinner we made a batch of chocolate chip cookies. She was delighted to wander around the yard offering them to our visitors. The cookies became part of the Sunday night tradition that first summer, and occasionally someone at our church would mention they were coming over that night for the moonflower show and cookies.

I had purchased a wooden garden sign years earlier that had a sunflower and the word "Welcome" painted on it. One night shortly before moonflower time, I got out the old sign and added the words, "If You Plant It—They Will Come" and pushed the sign into the dirt behind the plant.

And come they did. The grass in front of the plant became so worn that first summer that there were spaces where it was bare.

Some friends of ours occasionally used the plant to

bribe their children to get ready for bed on time. It's hard to settle kids down on long summer nights, so several times a week they would tell their kids that when they were all ready for bed, they would drive up to the Hall's to watch the moonflower. As soon as they pulled up in front of our house, the kids would jump out of their van in their summer pajamas, sometimes bringing their own blankets, and would snuggle with their parents as they waited for the plant to open at sunset on another hot summer day.

My next-door neighbor came with her camera and took beautiful pictures of the flowers. She was touched by the simple beauty of the plant and the fact that most people never saw it for what it really was, because it bloomed in the dark and faded with the morning sun. She suggested that I get a lawn chair or bench and leave it in front of the moonflower throughout the summer so that people could have a place to sit while they waited.

I searched for a garden bench and soon found what I wanted—a wrought iron and wood bench. We put the bench in front of the plant, facing it toward the street during the day and turning it around in the evening to face the moonflower. I soon noticed that I was digging up little clods of grass by constantly turning the heavy bench, so one night my husband suggested that we leave it facing the house. I told him it would look ridiculous. No one has a bench that faces the corner of their house. He reasoned with me saying, "People who know about the moonflower will know why it's facing that way, and no one else will even notice."

I should have known better.

# PART II

# The Lessons Begin

# The First Conversation

With the bench in place by the moonflower, I found myself sitting there more frequently. After walking out to the mailbox to pick up the mail, I would often gravitate to the bench and sit down for a few minutes. Sometimes I felt as if I had been transported from my hectic life back to Conewango Valley. I would breathe in and out slowly and deeply when I remembered the peace and serenity of the Amish farms.

One afternoon I was sitting on the bench, counting the number of pods I thought would bloom that night. The thought occurred to me that I should call a friend who had mentioned to me several times that she wanted to see the plant bloom and invite her to come by that evening. I smiled as I realized how many people had been there in recent weeks to see what several called the "Amish plant." As I sat and reflected on this new gathering place, I seemed to clearly hear a voice.

"I'm so pleased you have shared me with so many of your friends," the voice said. I looked around, but no one was there. I sat back on the bench for a minute, and then I thought I heard the voice again. "It has been wonderful to watch you take time each night to stop and share your life with your friends," it said.

I leaned forward and stared at the plant. I had lightheartedly talked to my plants many times, but was it possible the moonflower was talking to me? The thought was preposterous, but I felt in my heart that it was.

"Well . . . it's really not me they are coming to see," I said slowly. "But I have enjoyed visiting with my friends when they come to see you. I haven't had such leisurely conversations with them in years."

"Why is that?" the plant seemed to ask.

I sat back on the bench and thought for a moment. I

knew a plant couldn't really talk, but somehow I found myself drawn into the conversation as if I were talking with a dear friend.

"I—I don't know," I stammered.

"Well, think about it a while," the plant seemed to respond.

A few minutes later, I said, "I guess I always think there is too much to do and I don't have time to just sit and chat. I have worked full time ever since all my children were grown. We have a large family and many grandchildren. There are so many things I want to do, so many people that need my help, and so many places I need to be that I rarely take the time to sit in my yard and visit."

"What has changed to help you decide that you do have time to sit and visit?"

Before answering I thought about the events of the summer and of my many years of struggling with Attention Deficit Disorder.

"It has been a slow process," I said. "From my earliest childhood I have struggled with not being able to focus on something for very long or to sit quietly for more than just a few minutes. In a millisecond my brain darts from one thought process to something completely unrelated, and then to another, and another. Often those thoughts remind me of something I need to do, so I jump up and take care of it before I forget.

"Many times I have been in the middle of a conversation with someone when my mind has darted off to a completely unrelated subject, and then it darts off somewhere else. Several minutes later I would realize that I had missed half of what someone just told me.

"But with you," I said to the plant in almost a whisper, "I am different. When I am with you I feel calm, my breathing slows, and I can sit and think. I am able to focus on one thought for a long while, and I don't feel a need to jump up and do something else."

"The time I have spent just sitting and waiting for you to bloom has actually brought great joy into my life. I have reconnected with dear friends and have had wonderful, unhurried, and meaningful conversations with my husband, children, and grandchildren."

We were both quiet for a few minutes, and I finally stood up to go into the house. I leaned over the plant for a moment and brushed my hand across some of its leaves.

"I am so glad you came into my life," I said softly. "I've felt more peaceful with you nearby, and I learn so much when I sit quietly with you."

"That's why I came," the plant replied to my heart. "I have much to share with you, and I have all the time you need."

# The Bench That Faces the House

$O$ ne afternoon, while shopping at a grocery store, I ran into a friend I hadn't seen in months. We stopped and visited for a few minutes and caught up on the events of each other's lives. As our conversation was concluding, she said to me, "I just have to ask you a question. Why does that bench by your flower bed face your house?"

I laughed and told her about the moonflower, how it only blooms at dusk, and how I wanted a place to sit and wait until it opened. I told her how the bench used to face the street, and I would turn it around every night at moonflower time and then turn it back again. I finally decided to just leave it facing the moonflower because I was digging up my lawn.

"Oh, well, now that you've explained it, it makes perfect sense," she said. "Every time my husband and I drive by we think it's crazy that your bench faces the corner of your house."

I invited her to come by some evening before dusk and sit on the bench with me and watch the show. She said she would and was glad I told her about the bench, because now she could tell her husband and her next-door neighbor (who also thought the bench facing the house was strange), and they wouldn't think we were so odd any more. I laughed, and we both continued our shopping.

Later that week, I was weeding the flower beds in the front of the house. When I got to the corner where the moonflower was, I stood up to move the bench back a little. I smiled as I remembered my friend in the grocery store who thought we were a little crazy. As I weeded the corner area, I told the plant about our conversation.

"That's a lesson a lot of people need to learn," the plant stated simply.

"What lesson is that?" I asked.

It answered me with its own question. "Do you ever make judgments about people when you don't know the whole story?"

"Of course," I replied. "I'm sure everyone does."

"How many times do you think your opinion would be different if you really understood the reasons why people do the things they do?"

I saw where this was going. "Probably a lot of the time," I replied.

The plant was quiet for a few minutes, and I thought about a woman I had met years earlier. When I first met her, I didn't like her all that well. I questioned some of the things she said and did and made assumptions about her that were not accurate. I have always been grateful that I didn't hold on to my original feelings about her, because my impressions were completely inaccurate and she has been a dear friend for years.

Finally the plant seemed to answer. "It's hard work to always try to see the best in others, to try to understand them and accept the things they do. There is much about others you don't know anything about—experiences from their lives that have shaped their thinking and habits. If you could have insight into their lives, into their thoughts, fears, concerns, and insecurities, you would find that you could truly empathize with them, and many of your opinions would soften.

"When you meet people who do things or think differently than you do, it's easy to assume that your way is the better way, but that isn't always true.

"Many situations require us to make absolute judgments about what we believe is right and wrong, but so much of the conflict in homes and neighborhoods comes from not understanding that there are many right ways of living and doing."

I knew immediately that what had just been communicated to me was true. I sat on the bench, and for the next few minutes, I tried to process all I had just learned.

"There are a lot of people who have a bench that faces their house," the plant said at length. "And when you find out why, it will make perfect sense."

# A Twenty-eight-bloom Day

One night in midsummer, the moonflower produced twenty-eight blossoms, which was a new record. We were astonished, as were our friends who dropped by with their children to watch the show. We clapped and cheered as the last blooms surpassed the previous record of twenty-three.

But the next night there were only seven blooms. I waited on the bench until everyone left and asked, "Were you worn out after your twenty-eight-bloom night?"

"Oh yes!" I felt the plant reply. "I had to rest." I sat quietly for a few minutes before the plant continued, "All living things need rest—especially after a big project. You can't keep up a twenty-eight-bloom pace for too long or you will wither."

I thought about what the plant was telling me. I had always prided myself on being able to handle several big projects at once, almost thriving on the energy of having a lot to do, with ideas firing in all directions. With a brain that worked like mine, ideas and projects constantly flashed through my mind like bolts of lightning in a lightning storm. It seemed I always had several projects that I couldn't wait to start.

"But I like having lots of twenty-eight-bloom days," I protested. "I like always having things to do and projects waiting in the wings."

"There's nothing wrong with twenty-eight-bloom days," the plant explained patiently, "as long as you are sure that you have days with only a few blossoms—or even no blossoms—from time to time."

"How do I know how often I need one?" I asked.

"Pay better attention and you will know."

A few weeks passed. It was a Saturday night, and I

felt exhausted as my husband and I finished the yard work. It had been an unusually busy week at my job, and I worked two twelve-hour days in a row. Two of the nights that week we helped move our son and his wife out of their apartment and in with us. They would stay with us for the next six weeks before leaving for graduate school.

"I'm so tired," I said to the plant as I sat down on the bench to rest.

"I know you are," it replied. "I felt it when you were mowing the lawn."

I let out a deep sigh and said simply, "Yeah." I sat quietly, wishing I had a little more energy to finish the day's tasks.

"You've had four or five twenty-eight-bloom days in a row this week," the plant observed. "Can you get some rest tomorrow?"

I laughed and said, "Oh, some, I guess. I teach Sunday School in the morning, but my lesson isn't quite ready. Then our children and their families are coming over for dinner in the late afternoon."

"What are you making for dinner?" the plant asked simply.

It was such an unusual question for the moonflower to ask, but I was long past questioning its motives and teaching methods.

"We're going to barbecue chicken, and I'm going to make several salads and some rolls," I responded.

The plant laughed. "That sounds like about twenty blooms to me," it said.

"It will be."

"Is anyone helping you?"

"My kids usually do," I said, sighing. "But several of our sons and their families have been out of town this weekend and won't be back until just before dinner. Another son and his wife had a new baby two weeks ago, and one of my daughters, who is always a big help, won't be coming this week. That means I'm actually doing most of the food myself."

The plant sighed. "You need to rest, Chris."

"I know."

"Do you think you could cook something easier tomorrow night?" it asked.

I thought about it a few seconds before responding. "Like what?"

"Think about it awhile," the plant suggested.

I sat back on the bench and thought about it a few more seconds. "I can't think of anything," I said.

"Just relax and think awhile longer," the plant suggested.

I sat quietly, and my racing brain slowly began to calm. After some time had passed, the plant ventured a question: "Why is it that you love having your family over for dinner on Sunday nights, Chris?"

I didn't need to think—my response was immediate. "I love having them all in the house together," I replied. "I love the laughter and the fun and everyone talking at once. I love all the little grandchildren running around and playing together, the girls putting on the princess dress-up costumes, and the boys building forts with all my extra blankets. They are so much fun to be with, and it fills me with joy when they are all here."

And then the plant asked me a surprising question. "Why do they love to come to your house?"

"They love to be together too, laughing and talking and letting the cousins all play together. It's fun for everyone," I replied.

"You haven't said anything about the food yet."

"Oh, well, sure, and they love to eat."

"It sounds like the food is of little consequence to your kids," the plant said gently.

"It probably is," I replied.

We sat quietly together for a few minutes before it spoke again to my heart.

"What would be the easiest thing for you to make for dinner tomorrow that would require the least amount of preparation?"

"Oh, I don't know," I responded. Then I laughed and said, "Probably grilled cheese sandwiches and a green salad."

"How many blooms would that be?" it asked.

"About five."

"Sounds about right to me," the plant said simply.

"Yeah," I replied. "You're probably right."

But later that night I went ahead and made the marinade for the chicken and started preparations for some of the salads for the next day. By 9:00 p.m. the next night, all of our children and their families had left, and my husband and I were finishing the last bit of clean up. I was tired and wished I had gone with toasted cheese sandwiches and spent the afternoon reading. I was almost finished cleaning out the sink when I heard the plant speak to me from outside of the house. I turned off the kitchen faucet and stood quietly.

"Sometimes hard lessons are learned best when you don't get it quite right the first few times," it said with kindness. "What did you really have the energy to give today, Chris?"

"Five blooms."

"And what did you try to produce?"

"About twenty-five," I said, laughing.

"Is there anything that would make you feel better right now?" it asked.

"A hot bath and my favorite music."

"Excellent," the plant replied. "Go and do that, and we'll talk more tomorrow."

Later that evening, I went out to say good-night to the plant.

"Thanks," I said as I sat down on the bench. "I feel so much better." I enjoyed the peace and calm for several minutes in the cool night air. Just before I got up, I leaned over the plant and said quietly, "I'm learning."

"I know," the plant replied. "That's what I'm here for."

# There Will Always Be Time for Me

*I* didn't want moonflower visitors one night. It had been a hectic day and my husband and I were sitting alone on the bench, talking quietly. I had been waiting for several weeks to talk to him about something that had been weighing on my mind, but every time we tried to talk we were interrupted. We couldn't seem to get a moment alone. Our son and his wife and their baby were staying with us for six weeks, and we loved having them, but we hadn't had much time to sit and talk with each other. We were finally alone, and as we sat together on the bench in the gathering darkness, I felt like it was the perfect time to talk with him.

"I'm so glad no one is here to see the moonflower tonight," I began. "There's something I have wanted to talk with you about for several weeks." He reached over and took my hand, and I knew I had his complete attention. At that very moment, a car pulled up in front of our house and four people jumped out. Two of them were friends who lived nearby in our neighborhood.

"Are we too late?" they asked, as they hurried across the lawn. I let out a quiet sigh and my husband gently squeezed my hand.

"No," I replied. "You're just in time." Then my heart opened as if to say, "Come! Come share this joy."

They gathered around as the first pod started to shake. Our new friends were in awe as the first blossom opened within seconds, followed by seven or eight more. Several more friends stopped by and we visited with them until nearly 10:00 p.m. A few minutes after they all left, our daughter-in-law returned home with our grandbaby. They were both tired, and the baby was fussy. Our son was working that night, so I got up and went into the house to help get the baby settled down.

My husband and I didn't get to have our talk that night, but I knew our conversation would hold for a few more days. It wasn't anything urgent. I had struggled for months with a problem and had some ideas I wanted to talk over with the one person in the world who really knew me, and loved me anyway! It was over a week before the opportunity presented itself again.

When the time finally came, our conversation came about naturally, and the words came out effortlessly. I knew my husband understood what I was saying. He shared some of his thoughts, which gave me much-needed counsel and direction. I could not imagine it unfolding more perfectly.

It was late that night before I got a chance to sit down alone on the bench. I waited to see if the plant had anything to teach me, and after a few minutes, it spoke once again to my heart.

"There will always be time for you," it said gently. "There will always be time for your needs to be met. Ask for what you need, and then be willing to wait patiently. Sometimes you will have to wait longer than you want, but don't try to rush the process. Everything will unfold in perfect time. It might not seem that way at the moment, and you might be tempted to ignore the glaring needs of others to take care of smaller needs for yourself. But trust in this law of the universe—for as long as you are giving and helping with a genuine and loving heart, there will always be time for you."

Our conversation was interrupted by the sound of the baby crying. I sighed. I felt I should go in and offer to help, but I didn't want to move. I just wanted to sit and think and hear what the plant had to say to me, and I *didn't* want to do it another day. I wanted to understand more about how my needs could be met if I wasn't the one making sure they were. I sat for another minute or two as our grandbaby cried, and then the irony—almost the hilarity—of the situation struck me. I had just been taught a profound lesson and was already second-guessing it.

I laughed out loud, took a deep breath from the cooling night air, and went in to rock the baby. There would be time to finish our conversation another night.

# Bloom When You're Ready

Early one evening, I sat down by the plant, counting the pods I thought would open that night. I was sure there would be nine, but when they finally started to open I was surprised that there were only eight. The last one looked full, just like they always did before opening, but nothing happened. Several family members were there and kept encouraging it, but after about twenty minutes they all gave up and went into the house. I was about to join them, when I noticed the last pod starting to shake.

"Ohhh," I said, "do you want to open after all?"

It shook for about ten seconds, but again, nothing happened. I sat back on the bench and waited with it. It was now completely dark, long past the blooming time. The stalk began to shake back and forth. "Here it comes," I thought, but nothing happened. Over and over it would shake back and forth, then rest for a few minutes and begin again. Despite the fact that I had several things that really needed to be done that night, I found myself completely calm and my mind focused intently on my little friend.

I watched it struggle for over half an hour before I finally got down off the bench, knelt on the grass in front of it, and began to encourage it.

"You can do it," I said gently. "I know you can." Then, after thinking about my words for a minute, I changed them. "You can bloom whenever you want to," I said, "tonight, tomorrow, or whenever it's best for you. Bloom when you're ready."

There was something vaguely familiar about what I had just told the moonflower, and I smiled as the memory became clear. Many years earlier, on another warm summer evening, one of our sons and his fiancé thought it would be fun to go bungee jumping. Before long, all of our kids wanted to join them.

I had recently completed a ropes course with the youth from our church and was feeling adventurous and brave, so when they asked me to join them, I agreed. My younger children were surprised that I said I would go, but there was no question in my mind that I would actually jump.

When we arrived at the bungee tower, I paid the fee, got my equipment, and climbed to the top. It was much taller than it looked from the ground, and as I stepped onto the platform, I felt a wave of fear wash over me. I had made a big deal in front of my kids that I would do this. One of them said I would never jump, and I had replied, "Just get your camera ready!" And now they were all waiting below with video cameras in hand, ready to capture this historic moment.

But I couldn't do it. Time and again I walked to the edge of the platform and tried to get enough courage to jump, but after a few minutes, I would step back and let others take their turn. After twenty minutes of this, I too, was pretty sure I wouldn't jump.

There was a young woman working the tower that night who, for some reason, took a special interest in me. She called for another employee to come to the top and help the others. There were four platforms from which you could jump, but they were using only two that night. She took me to the third platform and asked, "Do you really want to do this?"

"Yes," I answered, "I really do."

"Why?" she asked.

"I don't know," I replied slowly. "But I do. I finished a ropes course a while ago and did some pretty challenging things. I even jumped off the eagle's perch! I thought this would be easy, but it's so much higher than it looks!"

"Yeah," the young woman said, laughing. "Almost everyone says that the first time they get up here."

"Is it okay if I sit down on the platform and then jump from there?" I asked nervously.

"Sure," she replied. "That helps a lot of people the first time."

I sat down on the floor and slowly inched my way to the edge of the platform and carefully slid my legs over the edge. My heart was pounding and my stomach was churning. Why on earth did people think this was fun? My children, who had long since put down their cameras and returned to jumping, were doing all kinds of tricks as they went off the various levels—frontward, backward, even doing somersaults off the platforms.

The young woman knelt down behind me and began asking about my children, who she noticed had kept cheering me on. We chatted a few minutes, and I asked her if she was still in school. She replied that she was a sports psychology major at a nearby university, and I asked her if she knew any psychology tricks she could use on me.

She laughed and told me not to worry. Then she said, "I know you will jump when you're ready. It might take you a little longer than it does for other people. But you know what's best for you, and you'll jump when you're ready."

Her words seemed to calm me, and my stomach

began to settle down. I was a little surprised that she was willing to spend this amount of time with me. "Are you afraid of heights?" she asked. "Are you worried you might get hurt?"

"No," I answered, "Not really."

After talking with me for probably another ten minutes, she asked a very interesting question. "Chris," she said gently, "Do you have any unresolved issues of fear or trust left from your childhood?"

I was startled by such a direct question from a stranger and even more surprised when tears filled my eyes, and I nodded my head.

She put her arm around my shoulder and said quietly, "If you decide to jump tonight, keep that fear in the front of your mind, take it with you when you jump, and let it go." She stood up and walked over to where another attendant was working, spoke to him for a moment, and then turned and looked back at me. She must have sensed my growing resolve, because she smiled and nodded her head in understanding.

From somewhere deep in my soul a voice said, "You

can do this. You will be safe. Let go." And with that unresolved fear fixed clearly in my mind, I slid off the tower. I screamed all the way down and was completely unprepared for the force that would yank me back up and drop me again and again. My screams gave way to sobbing, and I could hear my children cheering and clapping as the bouncing finally slowed, and I was lowered to the net. My sons bounded onto the net to help release me and they couldn't stop hugging me.

They were all talking and laughing at once, and told me that once they saw me sit down on the platform, they didn't really think I would ever jump. They kept saying they were so proud of me! My oldest son said, "Do you want to do it again, Mom?"

"No!" I replied, "Never! I don't need to. Once was enough!" Two of my sons put their arms around me and practically lifted me off the net to be greeted by the hugs of my other waiting children and friends.

"Way to go, Mom!" one shouted. Another one laughed and said, "It felt like forever before you finally jumped!" I knew exactly what she meant.

As my bungee jumping memory faded, and I found myself alone again with the moonflower, I repeated my words of encouragement. "Bloom when you're ready," I said and sat quietly as it struggled several more times to open.

A few minutes before 10:00 p.m., almost a full hour after the rest of the flowers had blossomed, the last one was finally ready. It burst open, every bit as beautiful as the rest. We had never had one bloom so much later than the rest, and I was pleased I had stayed long enough to see it. The plant's fan club that night was all but gone, but it bloomed just the same.

I sat on the grass, close to the plant, for a long while. It had not said a word, but the lesson was absolutely clear. We do not have to bloom when everyone else does. We do not have to do things or accomplish goals on anyone else's timetable in order for our life to unfold in perfect order. What is important is that we pay attention to all the signals we receive so we can bloom when the time is right for us. All that really matters is that when our time comes, we draw on the strength and courage that have been in us forever, let go of our mortal fears, and jump.

"Way to go," I said tenderly as I patted its leaves. "I know exactly how you feel."

# I Spent Third Grade In the Hall

"I have Attention Deficient Disorder," I confessed to the plant one morning.

"I know," the plant replied. "You have had it your whole life."

Tears filled my eyes.

"Why does that upset you so?" it asked me gently.

"Because it has caused me pain and embarrassment my entire life," I replied as memories of humiliating childhood experiences flooded my mind. I now understood that many of those experiences were a result of ADD and ADHD. The pain of such memories always made me push them from my mind, but this time was different. I became aware that I was consciously allowing myself to reflect on those experiences, which I rarely did. I felt no judgment, no ridicule, and no exasperation from my trusted friend, so I let the memories continue until they brought me back to the present.

"For many years I didn't understand why I struggled in so many areas of my life when none of my friends did. When I finally became aware that I had ADD, it was very hard for me to accept."

"Tell me about it," the plant said simply. "Take all the time you need." It waited patiently until I was ready to respond.

"Wow," I finally said. "I don't even know where to start." I sat quietly trying to figure out how to word what I wanted to say. "My brain often feels disorganized, and it is hard for me to focus on something for more than a few minutes at a time. The slightest sights and sounds easily distract me. Sometimes I have so many ideas popping into my mind at the same time that I feel that my brain is a pack of wild horses pulling a stagecoach. I am the stage driver, trying hard to hold the reins so I can stay on course. It seems I barely get back on track when another completely unrelated idea comes to me, and I'm off course again. For years, my life was a string of ideas—some of them great projects—that were started but never finished before a new idea took their place.

I sat quietly for a few minutes and the plant was quiet too. I had finally shared something I had never told anyone, with the exception of my husband and my doctor.

"I grew up feeling ashamed of the way I was. No one ever spoke of ADD when I was a child. I didn't know why I was different, but I did know I wasn't like everyone else."

"Why did you feel ashamed?"

"Because I was constantly in trouble," I replied without hesitation. "I think I spent most of my third-grade school year sitting on a chair in the hall. I could never sit still in class. I was always jumping around, talking out of turn, making silly comments, and never getting my work done. I could be distracted from my schoolwork with the slightest sound or movement in the classroom, and then it was difficult for me to settle down and get back to work. My teacher couldn't handle me. She would get so upset that she would put me on a chair in the hall, sometimes several times a day. Sometimes my mom would find out, and I would be in trouble when I got home. Then, at dinner, my mom would tell my dad, and it started all over again.

"I was continually reprimanded because I couldn't stay on task for two minutes—not at home or at school. I couldn't keep my schoolwork organized, my desk in order, or my bedroom clean, no matter how hard I tried or how much I was punished. My teachers frequently told me that if I would just try harder, I could settle down and do my work. I really did try, but after a few minutes, something would distract me, and I would be off-task again. A favorite comment on numerous report cards through grade school was, 'She has tremendous energy—if we could just get it channeled.'

"When I was in high school, I would watch my older sister as she struggled to learn Latin. She would often sit at her desk for two hours, memorizing and studying.

I could never sit at my desk for more than five minutes before I would think of something else I needed to do. I would wander away from my homework, and it would be an hour or more before I got back to it. It's a wonder I ever graduated, but I did, and then I went away to college.

"Eventually I met and fell in love with my husband, and we were married. But the problems continued for many years. I worked so hard to keep up, but an orderly home seemed the most elusive thing in the world to me. I watched other women around me and couldn't understand how they were so organized when my life seemed to be in constant confusion. Trying to hide my disorganization from the world was one of the most exhausting things in my life.

"But your home is not like that now," the plant replied.

"No, it's not."

"How did you change it?"

"I guess it began to change about ten years ago when I finally acknowledged that I had been struggling with

Attention Deficit Disorder my entire life. I wondered about it for years but wouldn't allow myself to consider it. A negative stigma was attached to ADD, and I couldn't accept that it might really be my problem. Eventually I talked to a trusted doctor about my struggles, and she sent me to a specialist for tests. My fears were confirmed, but the diagnosis had an interesting effect on me. Finally putting a name to my struggles gave me hope that there was a way to overcome them."

I sat quietly for a few minutes before the plant spoke again.

"Are you cured now?"

"No," I said, laughing, "but I am much better in so many ways."

"How did that happen?"

I settled back on the bench and thought about it for a few minutes. "Well," I said, "I realized I needed help. If sheer willpower and determination had been all that was required, I would have mastered my struggles years earlier. I started reading and studying every book I could find that dealt with ADD and learning how to manage it. I began watching for magazine articles on organizing a home. I took notes on everything and started implementing some of the ideas into my home and life.

"One day while I was reading, a remarkable thing happened. My mind became absolutely clear as to how all the extra 'stuff' in my house was affecting my brain and my thinking processes, prohibiting me from feeling the calm I longed for.

"It wasn't actually something in the book I was reading at the time. I had an epiphany, and I clearly understood part of my struggle. Many people can keep order regardless of how much they have in their home and their life, but I wasn't one of them. My already cluttered brain needed simplicity, in every area of my life. I knew exactly what I had to do, and I envisioned what my home would look like when I was done. I realized with absolute clarity that I needed space for everything to be visible, without stacking things on top of each other or behind other things.

"I went through every room in our house and got rid

of every item I hadn't used in the last year. I scaled down the contents of every room, closet, drawer, and storage space. It took months to complete, but I stayed with it, and I eventually began to see order and organization throughout our home. Occasionally I realized I had streamlined just a little too much when my husband or one of the children would ask where something was and I realized I had given it to a thrift store.

"I didn't automatically think of a logical place for each item, so I collected magazine articles on how to organize everything from a drawer to a closet. Once I saw a picture of how to do it, I could copy it exactly. I learned that if I didn't designate a specific place for every item, I would put things anywhere—out of sight, out of mind. Many times in the past, the surfaces would be clean, but the closets and drawers were a mess. As soon as I finished dejunking and organizing the entire house, order grew out of the chaos, and I discovered something about myself: I actually long for order."

The plant was silent for a minute, and then it asked me a profound question. "Is that why you love the

Amish so much, because of their ordered lifestyle?"

"It's one of many reasons," I replied.

"So," the plant concluded, "You found a way to create peace and order in your home and life by eliminating those things you don't really need and having a specific place for everything else."

"Exactly," I replied. "The hardest part is that I can never let my guard down. If I do, it seems that everything comes crashing down on me again. The peace leaves and the confusion returns. When that happens, I know what I need to do to get back on course.

"I had to squarely face the reality that my brain does not work like other people's. I have had to develop strategies to help me accomplish what I needed to do in order to be successful. I have Attention Deficit Disorder. It is a reality, but it doesn't have to be a bad thing. Yes, I'm easily distracted. It's hard for me to focus and it's hard for me to stay on task. If I don't constantly write things down, I can forget what I thought of thirty seconds ago. I keep a pad of paper nearby at all times in case an inspired thought flashes through my mind. But I am also creative and a pretty good problem solver. I truly believe there is a workable solution to just about every problem imaginable. I see joy and delight in so much of life, and I am generally quite happy.

"I know there are many things more difficult to deal with than ADD, but it has been a battle for me my entire life. It has affected how I felt about myself for many years."

I sat for a few minutes before sharing one last detail. "When I sit with you," I whispered, "quietly waiting for you to bloom, I feel calm and my mind is clear. The thoughts that come to me fill me with peace and hope. In those moments, I know there is time for me to do everything and become everything that I need to."

The plant said nothing for several minutes, and I had about decided to go back into the house when it taught me this lesson: "Did you know, Chris, that order is a fundamental law of the universe? There is a price you must pay for it, but it will always bring you peace."

"I'm learning that," I said.

"You've learned much," the plant replied.

# Questions

"Why do you always teach me things by asking me questions?" I asked the plant one night.
"Why do *you* think?" the plant responded.
"Because the answers are inside me," I said.
"Exactly," the plant replied.

# The Answers Are Inside You

Summer was coming to a close. I awoke early one morning in late August and went out to sit on the bench. The blossoms were still full in the early morning light, and I sat there quietly for about ten minutes before the moonflower spoke to my heart.

"Chris," the plant began, "you know I don't really talk to you, don't you?"

I smiled and nodded my head.

"The answers to your questions have always been inside you," it continued. "They were planted in your soul long before you were born. I just provided you with a reason to sit and wait quietly until you remembered and figured things out."

I asked my first question of the day, "But why didn't I learn some of these things earlier? Why didn't I learn these lessons before I met you, and why do I feel such peace when I sit here with you?"

The plant was still for a moment and then replied, "You have been learning and remembering great truths all your life, but there were some missing pieces that you learned while sitting with me. You linked that learning to a profoundly emotional experience that you had at your grandmother's farm. You and your husband and children traveled thousands of miles that first summer to gather with your family and clean out the farmhouse. That farm had been part of your family's experience and your dad's and your grandmother's life experiences for over one hundred years. You felt their presence that week as you worked together with love in cleaning, sorting, and dividing the memories of your past.

"The Amish you have always loved, who have been a big part of your family's history, were part of your life every day that week, assisting your family by bringing their wagons, water, and food. Then came that wonderful night when Marissa invited you to her home to see her moonflower bloom. You watched in amazement as the miracle began. It wasn't just her plant that drew you in; it was watching Marissa and her children—teenagers and young toddlers alike—clap with joy as each blossom unfolded. You had never seen anything like it—her plant or the Amish's joy at such simplicity.

"When Marissa offered to dig up some plants for you, you now had a tangible link to the love and joy you experienced with your family at the farm, and to the simplicity you so yearned for in your own life. You began to ask questions when you were sitting alone, waiting for me to bloom. And in that quiet stillness, the answers came. The miracle you experienced each summer since then was never about me. It's always been what you discovered about yourself and others when you realized that you really do have time to stop, sit quietly, focus, and reflect."

I sat completely still as I thought about today's lesson.

I finally decided to share what I had been thinking about for several days. "Summer is almost over," I said with emotion. "It won't be long before you will have blossomed for the last time this year and we will put the bench away for the winter." The plant didn't answer, so I leaned over, patted it gently, and said, "I will miss sitting here and learning from you."

"You can talk with me any time you want," the plant said, seeming to understand exactly what I was saying. "Anytime, and in any season. The answers will come if you sit quietly, ask your questions, patiently wait, and listen."

As I walked into the house, I reflected on the sequence of events that had brought this most unusual teacher into my life, and I was overwhelmed with love for my grandmother, who I felt had urged me to go to Marissa's farm that night years earlier to see the moonflower. Oh, what I would have missed if I had not listened!

# Exactly as I Am

*I*t was late September and the plant had not bloomed for days, but I still had one unanswered question, and I felt a sense of urgency to have it answered before winter set in.

The air that day was saturated with the wonderful, crisp smell of autumn, and leaves were already beginning to fall from our trees. Three of our grandsons had been over all afternoon, helping me clean out the flower beds. After they left, I sat down on the bench to rest and thought about the question I wanted to ask the moonflower. I didn't know exactly how to word it, but I finally decided to just ask and trust that it would understand my heart.

"Have you ever wished you were different?" I finally ventured.

"Like what?" the plant responded.

"Well, like a flower that smelled really beautiful, or one that bloomed in the day when everyone could see you. Not many people know anything about a moonflower unless they happen to come by at sunset when you are blooming. They never know how enchanting you are. I just wondered if you have ever wished that you were a rose, or a lily, or even a daisy."

The plant was quiet for several minutes, but when it answered, its voice was thoughtful and gentle.

"It has never occurred to me to try to be anything but what I am," the plant began. "I know who and what I am. I know better than anyone what I can do and be. I wasn't created to have an intoxicating smell that would become perfume, or to be used in floral arrangements that would grace the most joyful and sorrowful occasions in people's lives. I was created to instill a sense of wonder in those who come my way, to help them slow down, ask questions, and listen. I know who I am and what my work is. I am a unique and amazing creation, and I have much to share exactly as I am."

I let out a deep sigh. I knew what the plant was trying to teach me. Tears filled my eyes, and I felt a warmth wash over me as if someone had just wrapped a blanket around my shoulders. I sat quietly as images and thoughts went through my mind about who and what I am, what I am not, and what my life is really about.

I played the cello for several years in school, but I am certainly not a cellist. I can sing a strong alto, but I would never be considered a soloist. I can sew, but I'm not really a seamstress. I can cook but I am not a chef. What am I?

"It has never occurred to me to try to be anything but what I am and what I was created to be," the plant had said. Could it really be that easy? And then the familiar voice continued.

"You have *always* known who you are and what your life is about. But early in your childhood, you let the voices of those who didn't understand your struggles and were frustrated with your behavior cloud your vision and jam the signals coming from your soul until you forgot what you had once known. You began to believe things about yourself that were not true. When you are ready, you can let that part of your life be over. You don't have to hold on to any of those inaccurate beliefs another minute. You can let them go."

I breathed deeply several times and began to feel the heaviness around my heart lighten. I sat for a long while, thinking about all I had just been taught. When I finally looked at my watch, I realized that nearly an hour had passed. I wondered if the plant had anything else to say.

Several more minutes passed, and I finally stood up to go in the house. Just then, in the most tender and quiet voice, I heard it whisper something so familiar:

"You can bloom whenever you want to, Chris—tonight, tomorrow—whenever it's best for you. Bloom when you're ready."

"I think I'm ready," I said quietly and walked back into the house.

# An Instrument

The moonflower never changed. No matter how many people came to watch it, and regardless of how many came back on subsequent nights and brought their friends and oohed and aahed and clapped, it never changed. If it bloomed, it always bloomed at dusk with its beautiful flowers gracing the corner of our house all night. Then, in the morning light, the moonflowers always began to fade. It had much to share, and when I would ask a question, it would answer me slowly, giving me small pieces of information at a time, often asking me questions designed to get me to think.

"The answers are inside you," it would often say.

And when I protested that I couldn't think of the right answer, it would reply gently, "Think harder."

It reminded me of something I have always known—that everything I had been through and everything I had ever learned had given me experience and been for my good. Most important, those experiences were leading me in my life's work.

"What do you think your life's work is?" the plant asked me one night. I sat and thought about it for a long while before responding. "I think part of it," I began, "is to help others see their worth and to understand the goodness of their own lives."

"And what is it you want most to do with your life?"

I sat for a long while, trying to find the words that would best describe my feelings, when the words of a poem by St. Francis of Assisi came to my mind.

"Lord, make me an instrument of thy peace.
Where there is hatred, let me sow love;
Where there is doubt, faith;
Where there is despair, hope;

Where there is darkness, light;
Where there is sadness, joy."

Tears filled my eyes as I thought about what I most wanted to do with my life. Several minutes passed before I realized that St. Francis's poem was part of my answer. I whispered almost inaudibly, "I want to be an instrument in His hands."

The air was heavy with emotion, and once again, I felt as if I had been covered with a soft, warm blanket. I sat alone in the dark, weeping, yet filled with love and hope as I realized that I had just expressed what I really wanted to do with the rest of my life.

# PART III

## The Reason

# The Final Question

It was early October, and the plant had not bloomed for two weeks. But there was something I had wanted to talk to it about for a while, so early one evening I went to the corner of my house and sat down on the grass beside it. After several minutes, I finally began.

"I'm writing a book," I said quietly, "and it's about you. Is that okay?"

"That's why I came," the plant responded.

"You came so I would write about our visits?" I asked.

"Yes," it responded gently.

"But I don't understand."

"Tell me what you have learned from our times

together these past few summers," it asked me patiently.

I sighed. How could I possibly explain all the lessons and insights this mentor had taught me?

"I have learned that the answers to my questions are inside me and have always been inside me. I just need to take the time to sit quietly, listen, and remember what I have always known."

"Excellent," the plant said. A few minutes passed before it spoke again. "What else have you learned?"

"I have learned that there will always be time for me and for my needs to be met, but that I have to ask for what I need and then wait patiently as the answers unfold. I have also learned that my needs will sometimes be met in ways I didn't expect."

I sat back on the grass, resting against the bench. I didn't feel any need to hurry, and so I let my mind wander back through the past few summers to various experiences and lessons I had learned from my wise and nurturing mentor.

"I have learned," I continued, "That it really is okay to have a five-bloom day, or even a no-bloom day. I remember when you taught me that all living things need to rest—even you! I wasn't sure in the beginning how I would know when I needed a five-bloom day. You told me to pay better attention. So I started paying better attention to the way I felt and what I needed, and I learned that when I have too many twenty-eight-bloom days in a row, I don't feel nearly as much joy in my life."

My legs were starting to get stiff from sitting on the grass for so long, so I stood up and stretched for a minute and then sat down on the bench. A memory came to me that made me laugh.

"Do you remember my friend in the grocery store who told me she thought we were crazy because our bench faced the house? That was one of the first lessons you ever taught me. I still remember the understanding that filled my heart when I realized that people don't have to do things or think things the way I do to be doing what's right for them."

I was quiet for a long while, reflecting on the sequence of events that had occurred, all in perfect order, and all in perfect timing, that had allowed me to learn these life lessons.

Finally, the plant spoke. "Is there anything else you have learned?" it asked quietly.

Tears filled my eyes as I realized I was about to share the most profound lesson the plant had ever taught me.

"I have learned . . ." I began, and then paused, searching for the words to express what was in my heart. "I have learned—or as you would say—I have remembered that, like you, I am unique and amazing, exactly as I am, and that I have much to share."

"ADD and all?" it asked gently.

"Yes," I responded with a smile.

"Tell me about that," the plant requested.

I sighed. I didn't know how to explain the change that had occurred in me over the last several summers. It had created a freedom in me that allowed me to feel normal and finally be able to talk openly and honestly about my challenges with ADD. For me to actually be able to laugh about something that had previously brought only pain and embarrassment to me throughout my life was a great gift. A giant weight had been lifted now that I no longer felt I had to try to hide my struggles.

As I sat reflecting, I thought back to an afternoon many years earlier when one of my sons came in the kitchen. He laughed and said, "Hey Mom, I heard a joke at school today. Do you know how many people with ADD it takes to change a light bulb?"

"No," I said. "How many?"

But before the words were even out of my mouth, he interrupted me saying, "You wanna go ride bikes? Oh look, a shiny thing!" We both laughed together that day, but the joke was *really* funny to me now, because I could openly admit that I see shiny things everywhere, everyday.

"That *is* funny," the plant said, interrupting my thoughts.

"What?" I asked.

"That joke about the shiny things," it responded.

"You knew what I was thinking? You know my thoughts?" I asked incredulously.

113

"Of course I do," it answered gently. "I know everything about you. I know what you have been through, what you have learned, and what you still need to learn. I know what you have forgotten and what you still need to remember.

"You have always been unique and amazing exactly as you are," the plant continued. "But for many years you let other voices convince you otherwise. All I did was provide you with a reason to sit, unhurried, until you could remember who you are and what you have always known."

I felt so loved and understood in that moment that I couldn't speak. Once again I was filled with a sense of wonder for the events that had transpired at my grandmother's farm and brought this insightful teacher into my life.

"Do you think there are others who have also forgotten who they are and what their lives are really about?" the plant asked at length.

"Absolutely," I replied.

"I think so too," it answered to my heart.

I sat and thought for a while and finally said, "But not everyone has a moonflower."

"That's true," the plant responded. "But not everyone needs one. You did. You needed something that would slow you down and give you a reason to sit quietly. When you started to really listen, you began to hear the answers you were seeking."

We sat quietly for several minutes before the plant went on. "Everyone needs to learn how to get answers to their questions. You have learned well that the answers don't always come as soon as you ask, but if you wait patiently, the answers will come. When people are ready to learn, when they are ready to ask, when they are ready to listen, their teacher will come."

"Will you be back in the spring?" I asked as tears filled my eyes.

"I will be here all winter," the plant replied.

"Under the snow?"

"Under the snow, in the rain, in the sun . . . I will always be here."

"Thank you for coming to me," I finally managed to whisper. "You have changed my life."

"You were ready to change your life," the plant concluded tenderly. "That's why I came."

To receive your free packet of seeds, visit www.conversationswithamoonflower.com.

## How to Care for Your Moonflowers

Name: Oenothera biennis

Planting: No pre-treatment needed. Sow seeds just below soil surface at 70$^0$F and water.

Color and type: Yellow biennial

Bloom time: Summer

Light: Full sun to part shade

Height: 24" to 60"

Spacing: 15" to 18"

Soil: Medium to dry

Water: Average moisture

Fertilizer requirements: 2–3 times over the summer

Special instructions: Guard against snails and caterpillars. They seem to love the moonflowers even more than you will!

Author's note: There are a variety of night-blooming moonflowers. Oenothera biennis may vary from those described in the book.

# To Maximize Your Enjoyment of Your Moonflower Plant

Place several lawn chairs in front of the plant about ten to fifteen minutes before the normal blooming time. You can either sit quietly by yourself or invite a family member or neighbor to share the joy with you. Pay attention to your thoughts as you sit peacefully in the twilight waiting for each blossom to open. Breathe deeply. Ask questions. Listen. After the plant has finished blooming, sit quietly a few more minutes. Reflect on your blessings. Breathe deeply. Listen a little longer.

Enjoying your moonflowers with popcorn or cookies is optional!

# *About the Author*

Chris Hall's creativity and energy were evident in her earliest childhood. Her grade school teachers often commented, "She has tremendous energy—if we could just get it channeled." Her parents instilled in her a belief that good can come from almost every experience, and that belief, along with an ability to see humor in much of everyday life, proved invaluable as she and her husband raised their eight children.

Chris has been a presenter for many years for Franklin/Covey's *The 7 Habits of Highly Effective Families, Becoming a Love and Logic Parent,* and *Becoming a Love and Logic Teacher.* The gift of a moonflower plant that she received from one of her grandmother's Amish neighbors resulted in *Conversations with a Moonflower,* her first published work.

Now empty nesters, she and her husband, Duane, find great joy in spending time with their children and grandchildren. They are still amazed upon returning home from work each night to find the kitchen has remained clean all day.